A Bill's Journey into Law

by Suzanne Slade

illustrated by Tony Trimmer

HR - 1000

PICTURE WINDOW BOOKS

a capstone imprint

Special thanks to our advisers for their expertise:
Betsy Sinclair, PhD, Assistant Professor of Political Science
University of Chicago

Terry Flaherty, PhD, Professor of English
Minnesota State University, Mankato

Editor: Jill Kalz
Designer: Tracy Davies
Art Director: Nathan Gassman
Production Specialist: Sarah Bennett
The illustrations in this book were created with mixed media/found object.

Picture Window Books
151 Good Counsel Drive
P.O. Box 669
Mankato, MN 56002-0669
877-845-8392
www.capstonepub.com

All books published by Picture Window Books are manufactured
with paper containing at least 10 percent post-consumer waste.

Library of Congress Cataloging-in-Publication Data
Slade, Suzanne.
 A bill's journey into law / by Suzanne Slade ; illustrated by Tony
Trimmer.
     p. cm. — (Follow It!)
 Includes index.
 ISBN 978-1-4048-6831-1 (library binding)
 ISBN 978-1-4048-7027-7 (paperback)
 1. Bill drafting—United States—Juvenile literature. 2.
Legislation—United States—Juvenile literature. 3. Legislative
bodies—United States—Juvenile literature. I. Trimmer, Tony. II.
Title.
 KF4950.S53 2012
 328.73'077—dc22   2011006500

Printed in the United States of America in North Mankato, Minnesota.
032011
006110CGF11

Today is Ramesh's favorite day of the year—his birthday.

Ramesh loves presents and cake. But he loves eating ice cream most of all. As he blows out the candles, Ramesh makes a special wish.

Ramesh thinks free ice cream would make lots of people happy. He wonders if his idea could become a law. He calls the congressperson who represents his state to find out.

The U.S. Congress makes laws for the country. Congress is run by two groups, the House of Representatives and the Senate. If a representative or senator agrees to sponsor an idea, it may be introduced as a bill. Then it has a chance of becoming a law.

The congressperson takes Ramesh's idea to the Capitol Building in Washington, D.C.

6

She types up the idea and turns it into a bill. The bill gets its own number.

The congressperson drops the bill into a wooden box called a hopper. Now the bill is ready to be introduced to Congress.

From idea to paper in no time flat!

HR - 1000

Thousands of new bills are introduced into Congress every year. Only about 4 percent become laws.

The House of Representatives has many committees that study new bills. Each committee specializes in certain areas, such as education or agriculture (farming). The Senate has its own committees that look at new bills.

After the group shares its ideas, the representatives vote. More than half vote yes, so the bill continues its journey.

The U.S. House of Representatives has 435 members. A bill needs more than half of the representatives to vote for it in order to pass.

11

The bill moves on to a Senate committee. Members look over the bill carefully. They ask more questions.

The senators think of questions no one has asked yet: How will we pay for all this free ice cream? Taxes? What about people who don't have an ice-cream shop nearby? Can someone get a rain check if she's sick on her birthday?

After many days, each senator votes. There are more "yeas" than "nays," so the bill keeps moving.

There are 100 senators in the U.S. Senate. Two are elected from each state. Like in the House, a majority must vote in favor of a bill for it to pass. In the Senate, "yea" means yes, and "nay" means no.

15

After passing the House and the Senate, the bill is printed on official paper. Two important people, the vice president of the United States and the Speaker of the House, sign the bill.

But the journey's not over yet! Next stop? The White House.

I'm so nervous. I'm going to meet the president!

A bill may have many changes, or amendments, during its journey to become a law. Both the House and the Senate must give the amendments the OK.

In his oval office, the president reads every word of the bill. He thinks about lots of things. Will this bill help people? Is it fair? How much will it cost?

If the president does not like a bill, he or she can veto it. A vetoed bill may still become law if two-thirds of the members in both the House of Representatives and Senate pass the bill again.

The president smiles and grabs a new pen.
He signs the bill and makes it a law.

Now Ramesh, and everyone else in the United States, will enjoy free birthday ice cream!

Diagram of a Bill's Journey

Idea

Sponsored by congressperson

Bill

Discussed and voted on by the House Committee

Discussed and voted on by the House of Representatives

Discussed and voted on by the Senate Committee

Discussed and voted on by the Senate

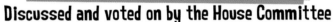

Vice president, Speaker of the House, and president sign the bill

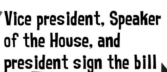

LAW

(Note: If the bill does not pass one of the voting sessions at any point, it "dies." It does not continue its journey.)

Glossary

amendment—a change made to a bill

committee—a group of people chosen to do certain work

elect—to choose someone as a leader by voting

House of Representatives—one of two houses in the U.S. Congress that makes laws; the House has 435 members, some from each state

representative—a person who is chosen to speak or act for someone else

Senate—one of two houses in the U.S. Congress that makes laws; the Senate has 100 members, two from each state

sponsor—to be responsible for

veto—to refuse or say no to

To Learn More

More Books to Read

Bright-Moore, Susan. *How Is a Law Passed?* Your Guide to Government. New York: Crabtree Pub. Company, 2009.

Fein, Eric. *The U.S. Congress.* Cartoon Nation. Mankato, Minn.: Capstone Press, 2008.

Scheppler, Bill. *How a Law Is Passed.* The U.S. Government: How It Works. New York: Chelsea House Publishers, 2007.

Taylor-Butler, Christine. *The Congress of the United States*. A True Book. New York: Children's Press, 2008.

Internet Sites

FactHound offers a safe, fun way to find Internet sites related to this book.
All of the sites on FactHound have been researched by our staff.

Here's all you do:
Visit *www.facthound.com*
Type in this code: 9781404868311

Super-cool stuff!

Check out projects, games and lots more at
www.capstonekids.com

Index

Look for all the books in the Follow It series:

A Bill's Journey into Law

A Dollar Bill's Journey

A Germ's Journey

A Monarch Butterfly's Journey

A Plastic Bottle's Journey

A Raindrop's Journey